That's Not a Pet!
CAN I HAVE A PET CROCODILE?

By Michou Franco

Please visit our website, www.garethstevens.com. For a free color catalog of all our high-quality books, call toll free 1-800-542-2595 or fax 1-877-542-2596.

Library of Congress Cataloging-in-Publication Data

Names: Franco, Michou, author.
Title: Can I have a pet crocodile? / Michou Franco.
Description: New York : Gareth Stevens Publishing, 2019. | Series: That's not a pet! | Includes index.
Identifiers: LCCN 2017040513| ISBN 9781538217801 (library bound) | ISBN 9781538217825 (pbk) | ISBN 9781538217832 (6 pack)
Subjects: LCSH: Crocodiles as pets–Juvenile literature.
Classification: LCC SF515.5.C75 F73 2018 | DDC 639.3/982–dc23 LC record available at https://lccn.loc.gov/2017040513

First Edition

Published in 2019 by
Gareth Stevens Publishing
111 East 14th Street, Suite 349
New York, NY 10003

Copyright © 2019 Gareth Stevens Publishing

Editor: Therese Shea
Designer: Sarah Liddell

Photo credits: Cover, p. 1 worananphoto/Shutterstock.com; p. 5 Ondrej Prosicky/Shutterstock.com; p. 7 Suptar/Shutterstock.com; p. 9 Ning Je taine/Shutterstock.com; p. 11 Wendy Nero/Shutterstock.com; p. 13 MRAORAOR/Shutterstock.com; pp. 15, 24 (nest) Ger Metselaar/Shutterstock.com; p. 17 Stuart G Porter/Shutterstock.com; p. 19 JMx Images/Shutterstock.com; p. 21 pattang/Shutterstock.com; p. 23 katacarix/Shutterstock.com; p. 24 (turtle) tawan/Shutterstock.com.

All rights reserved. No part of this book may be reproduced in any form without permission in writing from the publisher, except by a reviewer.

Printed in the United States of America

CPSIA compliance information: Batch #CS18GS: For further information contact Gareth Stevens, New York, New York at 1-800-542-2595.

Contents

A Pet Croc? 4

Croc Life 6

Hungry! 16

Not Safe! 20

Words to Know 24

Index 24

I want a pet.

I want a crocodile!

Crocodiles live in hot places.

They like to be in water.

They walk on land.
They run, too!

The sun helps crocodiles warm up.

Crocodiles make nests.
They use mud and leaves.
They lay eggs in nests!

Crocodiles eat fish. They eat turtles and birds, too.

Crocodiles hide in water. They surprise big animals on land!

Crocodiles aren't good pets.
They're not safe!

21

I'll visit them at the zoo!

Words to Know

nest

turtle

Index

land 10, 18

nests 14

sun 12

water 8, 18